PURPOSE

ALAN RAYMOND FINE

Prescott Publications

Prescott Publications
Minneapolis, Minnesota USA

Copyright © 2018 by Alan Raymond Fine

All rights reserved. No part of this book may be reproduced or transmitted in any form or by any means, electronic or mechanical, including photocopying, recording, or by any information storage and retrieval system, without permission in writing from the publisher or Alan Raymond Fine.

Published by Prescott Publications
P.O. Box 16083, Minneapolis, MN 55416

Printed in the United States of America

Library of Congress Cataloging-in-Publication Data

Fine, Alan Raymond

Purpose by Alan Raymond Fine — 1st Edition

This publication contemplates life meaning and purpose and seeks to provide the reader with inspiration toward building a better physical, emotional and spiritual self, a beautiful life, and a better world.

ISBN: 978-1-7329572-0-6

10 9 8 7 6 5 4 3 2 1   pbk.

First Edition

Author's Note

This work contemplates life purpose in poetry and message. It seeks to provide the reader with inspiration toward building a better physical, emotional and spiritual self, a beautiful life, and a better world. Included are reflections on moral duty, personal fortitude, teamwork and world betterment, faith, devotion, introspection and personal refinement, love and intimacy, enlightenment, and spiritual elevation.

Acknowledgment

To a work such as this, there are many contributors. A lifetime's worth, to be exact. For the development and production of the book itself, I feel a deep sense of gratitude to God, my parents and my children, to my greater family, to my teachers and friends, my work associates, my fellow human beings, and my life circumstances and experiences.

Dedication

This book is dedicated to those who read it, hoping it has a profound impact on how you see the world, and inspires you to aspire to be a better person, to build a better world through mindful action, and to live a life filled with richness.

About the Author

Alan Raymond Fine is currently founder and CEO of Elluette, a Minnesota General Benefit Corporation whose mission is to lead prosperous collaborations towards the health, harmony and security of the world. For more information, please visit www.elluette.com.

For decades, Mr. Fine has been transforming minds and organizations for the better. Seasoned in business, politics, philosophy, theology, music and wellness, he has share his insights, perspectives and creativity extensively with others.

His work with organizations includes coaching mindfully pragmatic and ethical leadership, assistance with the development of healthy and productive cultures, facilitation of compelling strategic plans, exploring methods to refine internal organization processes, and assistance with financings and mergers to support organizational development and growth. As a faculty member at the Carlson School of Management for nearly a quarter century, Mr. Fine has taught these principles to thousands of students.

Mr. Fine, also, is accomplished in the performing arts and athletics and has taken a multidimensional approach to spiritual, emotional and physical wellness research and practice.

Special Thanks

Special thanks:
- To God, for gracing me with the opportunity to live this life and walk this earth.

- To my mother, Beverlee, and my father, Ralph, to which there are no words that can describe my appreciation for all that they have done for me.

- To my son, Louis, and my daughter, Melania, for their love, patience, and support.

- To all my dear friends.

PURPOSE

ALAN **R**AYMOND **F**INE

Contents

A Timeless Millennium Message 5

Let Freedom Ring! 9

A Prayerful Lullaby of Faith 15

How Can I Say "I Love You?" 21

As You Are 25

My Refuge 31

Show Us a Glimpse of Divine 35

If 39

Cherish Her Whole 43

Time 47

If You are There 49

Touch the Sky 53

Children of Light 57

Valor 61

Higher 65

Time in the Sun 69

Purple Roses 73

The Dawn 77

Share with Me the Silence 79

The Promised Land 81

A Cool Spring Breeze 85
To Create a Work of Art 89
A Familiar Place 91

A Timeless Millennium Message

THOMAS JEFFERSON once said, *"Our greatest happiness does not depend on the condition of life in which chance has placed us, but is always the result of good conscience, good health, occupation, and freedom in all just pursuits."*

The founders of our beloved country were obsessed with the concept of a kinder world in which each individual would be equipped with the necessary freedoms to pursue happiness:

"We hold these Truths to be self- evident, that all [people] are created equal, that they are endowed by their Creator with certain unalienable Rights, that among these are Life, Liberty and the Pursuit of Happiness."[1]

This has been the quest of our country since the very beginning. Thomas Paine called this cause, in his Common Sense Pamphlet, *"...the cause of all [human]kind."*[2] This inspiration, this quest, regardless of station, is repeated inclusively throughout our land:

"Give me your tired, your poor, your huddled masses yearning to breathe free..."[3]

---

[1] Thomas Jefferson, *"The Declaration of Independence,"* July 4, 1776
[2] Thomas Paine, *"Common Sense Pamphlet,"* January 10, 1776
[3] Emma Lazarus, *"The New Colossus,"* 1883

A Timeless Millennium Message

While in its humble beginnings, the population of the United States of America was a mere 2.5 million people, by the middle of the 21st century, our country may approach a population 175 times larger. The tired, poor, huddled masses, have come, and continue to arrive. They have transformed our country into the most powerful nation on this planet--the envy of the world—not because of technological advancements, but because of the kind, just spirit that is our nation. A spirit that inspires every American to defend this freedom: The freedom to dream, and to live those just dreams with dignity.

A new century comes with unprecedented technological advancements that have transformed our lives. Advancements in global communications and transportation, over the last decade alone, have enabled the masses to interface in a multitude of forms and on an unprecedented scale. While this has wreaked havoc with cultural and national identity, these advancements coupled with the message of our prosperity, and our quest, has resulted in a world population yearning to "breathe free." A movement towards not just a borderless economy, but a borderless society defined by principles, not geography.

In other words, the visionary stance of the founders of our country has, as Thomas Paine once said, enabled the world to realize this truth and to make the *"cause of America,"* the *"cause of all [human]kind."*[4]

Note that technology alone has not changed the world. While it seems readily apparent that we will continue to be

---

[4] Thomas Paine, *Common Sense Pamphlet,* January 10, 1776

A Timeless Millennium Message

confronted with advances in technology, these technologies are only tools. In the hands of wicked people, these tools become methods for inducing chaos. In the hands of people of "good conscience," they become the tools of constructive change.

The quality of our character and that of our leadership, therefore, will reflect the quality of our future. While I am excited about the technological advancements that are forthcoming, I am concerned about the inheritors of these advancements.

Freedom is very fragile, it does not exist within a vacuum. It is a collaborative effort with principles laying a foundation upon which happiness can be pursued by all. I believe, however, that it can be weakened by egocentric and opportunistic leadership. Leadership that proposes
- to compromise integrity is to be human,
- to compromise personal principles is to be pragmatic,
- to speak of our faith in God as weak-minded is to be correct, and
- to desecrate our way of life is to be free.

Leadership that reminds me of the ancient story of the sailor who, sitting in a boat, begins drilling a hole in the floor. When confronted by others concerning his behavior, the sailor responds, "But, I am only drilling a whole under my seat." "Yes," they reply. "But, when the water rushes in, we will all drown!"

We need to ensure that the character of our leadership does not drill holes in the fabric of our society. Since this leadership is a reflection of our decision-making and our

A Timeless Millennium Message

character, in this new millennium, we need to refine ourselves if we are to become the role models that the future needs. We need to refine ourselves, so that we can understand how to improve the character of our leadership. We need to refine ourselves, if we hope to build a better world. We must strive to be people of "good conscience!" In effect, well-balanced people who hold ourselves, and our leaders, as trustees of the public good.

Martin Luther King, a shining light, wisely said, *"In the process of gaining our rightful place we must not be guilty of wrongful deeds. Let us not seek to satisfy our thirst for freedom by drinking from the cup of bitterness and hatred. We must forever conduct our struggle on the high place of dignity and discipline."*[5]

When the architects of our republic wrote the magnificent words of the Constitution and the Declaration of Independence, they were signing a promissory note to which every American was to fall heir. This note was a promise that all people would be guaranteed the inalienable rights of life, liberty, and the pursuit of happiness.

It is my belief that the message of Jefferson nearly two and a half centuries ago, to the words of King in the twentieth century, project the direction that we must all continue to take through this new millennium and beyond, not just as a nation, but as a world.

---

[5] Martin Luther King, *"I Have a Dream," Speech at the Lincoln Memorial,* August 28, 1963

Let Freedom Ring!

More than two hundred years ago—

    came forth a nation,

        A shining beacon—

            built on liberty;

The world would never be the same:

    We had our faith,

        We gave our lives,

            We pledged our love:

                Let Freedom Ring;

And now we live in liberty,

    Born free to pursue happiness:

        To live,

            To love,

                To dream,

                    To share,

LET FREEDOM RING

To give,

    To hope,

        To marry,

To build our children strong and free—

    in liberty,

        In love and prayer:

        One nation—

            under God;

In every generation—

    we must stand together,

        Holding these truths,

            Our rights forever;

To be born free,

    It's what we strive to be;

        As such,

            We must protect—

                life and liberty;

LET FREEDOM RING

We must stand strong,

    We must stand right,

        To sacrifice,

            To heed the call:

                Indivisible;

She needs us now—

    To make things right,

        To shine the light,

           To fight the fight:

                With liberty—

                    and justice—

                      for all;

Adventurers,

    Entrepreneurs,

        Educators,

            Liberators:

                A call to arms,

                    A call to you;

LET FREEDOM RING

A call old glory,
> For red, white and blue;

Medicine,
> The nano-world;

Space,
> Robots,
>> Sky farms,
>>> Dot coms;

Organic food,
> Renewables;

A world of beauty,
> Of species through and through,
>> A paradise of nature,
>>> Sustainably true;

With faith in God,
> We'll stay the course:
>> To end the strife,
>>> To build the peace;

Let Freedom Ring

To deliver prosperity,
    To lead the world;
To live,
    To love,
        To dream,
            To share;
To give,
    To hope,
        To marry;
To build our children strong and free,
    In liberty,
        In love and prayer:
            One nation,
                Under God,
                    Indivisible,
                        With liberty—
                            and justice—
                                for all;

LET FREEDOM RING

In this generation—

   we must stand together:

      Build a brighter future—

         with our own resources;

      With the strength of will,

         With resolve to win;

   To continue to be—

      the shining light—

         of liberty;

Of thee I sing,

      My allegiance do I pledge:

   Let Freedom Ring!

A Prayerful Lullaby of Faith

Moonlight,

    Snowflakes,

        Glistening in the night air;

            Where are we going?

                Where have we been?

            Who am I without You?

                Where did we begin?

See the trees—

    sway in the breeze,

        Their branches all clinging together;

A caterpillar,

    A butterfly,

The mysteries of life,

    Of wonders by and by;

A tapestry of color,

    Of musical wind and song;

A Prayerful Lullaby of Faith

Dreams of waters showering me—

    with warmth and sight for long;

A deer stands by Your flowers,

    Your life force fills my veins;

Dolphins soar from wave to wave,

    From sky, a heavenly refrain;

Through an effortless symphony of rainbows—

    The mourning doves ascend;

A lightning score rumbles my mind's eye—

    before water feeds Your fame;

The sky welcomes the sunrise,

    My spirit meets the dawn,

A morning stretch fills grateful lungs,

    My lips, a fragrant yawn;

Where ever You will lead me—

    I will trust Your path in faith,

A Prayerful Lullaby of Faith

And when I feel You're far away —
I will reckon from my place;

Whatever my misfortune —
Know that I am here,
I may complain about You,
But, it's only that I fear;

Death will come to me in time,
I know not where I'll go,
As long as You are with me —
I will trust You, to and fro;

All I ask for is Your mercy,
Your love and Your embrace,
So, please don't ever leave me,
Keep me company in my place;

And when the time is near —
For my mortal shell to shed,

A Prayerful Lullaby of Faith

Please wipe away my tender tears—

Help me to right my head;

Afraid, I am without You,

So escort me to Your door,

And when we reach Your heavens,

Please show me what is more;

Help me to see your wonders—

and make my spirit soar,

Invite me to your table—

for the truth stands evermore;

Help me find my loved ones,

Please bring them to my door,

Illuminate with Your sweet sun—

Your Spirit as before;

Help me to reach your garden,

Set a bench beside Your throne;

A Prayerful Lullaby of Faith

Fill me with sweet passions—

    with directions to my home;

Set me on a righteous course—

    and build my life anew,

        build within myself the source,

            Your Spirit, truth and true;

Guide me with your wisdom,

    Stand with me, unyielding lengths,

        Open up your Kingdom,

            Infuse me with great strengths;

Please don't ever leave me,

    Include me in Your show,

        Deliver me,

            Set me free,

                Summon me hither,

                    Make me glow!

How Can I Say "I Love You?"

How can I say "I love you?"
    What words can I use?

My song is my life,
    The music of my soul;

My every action,
    My every gesture,
        Sings to you;

My intellect and sincere respect—
    is deeply entranced with you;

Inspiring kindness of deeds,
    My altruism honors you;

The rivers of my life reach out to you,
    Extending to you my finger ring;

How Can I Say "I Love You?"

The key to my treasure,

    Brimming with pearls,

        Emeralds,

           Rubies—

                and diamonds,

                    pales by comparison—

                        to the glisten of your eyes;

A garland of soft colorful flowers,

    Adorned with tender strands—

        of silver and gold,

           Is yours for the taking—

                if you would merely—

                    extend to me—

                        your finger ring;

My nobility is inspired by you,

    Your elegance;

How Can I Say "I Love You?"

My mind is drawn to you,
    Your kindness;

My spirit clings to you,
    Your body's dance;

My heart yearns for you,
    Your glance;

My body aches for you,
    Your smile;

Because you are you,
    Your intellect,
        Your soft respect,
            Your glance,
                Your smile,
                    Your kindness too,
                        Your graceful dance,
                            Your elegance;

How Can I Say "I Love You?"

You make my spirit shine,

    You make my body glow,

You inspire me to grow—

    tall enough to stand beside you—

        like the sun that peers above the horizon,

            Illuminating the dawn!

As You Are

Look into another's eyes—

    and see the sun that shines inside:

        In the glimmer,

            In the sparkle,

                Of the windows of their soul;

In each pair resides a chest—

    of countless pains and joys:

        An endless sea of tales,

           A human score of love and lore,

                Of triumphs and disasters;

And don't forget—

    a mirror stands—

        to see your story too:

           In black and white,

                In color true;

                A tapestry of red and blue,

                    Of green and orange—

                      and yellow too;

As You Are

The past reflect,
    The future too,
        But, do not miss the present:
            Make rich your life,
                Each moment true —
                    with dreams, goals, plans,
                      Of triumphs tried,
                          Of love, don't hide;

And with mirror reflect,
    Your eyes will show —
        the good, the bad —
            and all that you had;

Take it in —
    with smile and grin,
        For the greatest story —
            is the story told —
                through picture windows whole;

As You Are

God gave you life,
    God gave you time,
        God set you in this paradigm:
            To shine,
                To sparkle,
                    To glimmer too;
            To be and see,
                To feel and hear;

The eyes they see,
    Record,
        Reflect,
            Connect,
                Depict,
                    The moments true;

And when you see,
    In mirror free,
        A life unfold—
            of legend and ode:

As You Are

Realize it's yours,

Your life you see,

A story to be lived —

with dignity;

So take this grand opportunity,

And compose a story that sets you free:

Live each moment in search of meaning;

Love until your heart is beaming;

Share it with those that love you dear:

And don't forget —

to stand up and cheer;

Be joyful and laugh from ear to ear —

for time will rush —

from year to year;

Before you know it —

the time will come,

For you to recall —

both sigh and hum;

As You Are

So—

    Cherish the days that you are granted,

        And live to the fullest,

            A life enchanted!

My Refuge

I've traveled far in search of fame:

    For pots of gold,

        For magic things;

    For dreams that vanish in the air,

        For songs of life that go nowhere;

I've searched my heart,

    I've searched my soul,

        I've struggled just to keep them whole;

And when the darkness stood its ground,

    I looked within—

        and found the sound—

            of You;

A voice of love ,

    A voice of pain,

        I know I couldn't hide my shame:

            I had to open up the door—

My Refuge

    and face myself—

        with You once more;

And as we moved into the light,

    The sound inside it beamed so bright:

        For darkness there was just despair,

            Together it could go nowhere;

I've never known a love that laughed and cried,

    Until I found You—

        standing by my side;

Deep in my heart,

    My rock, my refuge too,

        Awaiting my return—

            with threads of white and blue;

And when the sun began to set—

    Your footsteps did appear:

        The burdens that I carried long—

            began to disappear;

My Refuge

And now I know the answers too,

    the questions of my life;

        Never alone,

            I was at home,

                My Friend—

                    always sincere:

                        To guide me through—

                            a love that's true,

                                I didn't have to fear:

For truth be told,

    It was never cold—

        for You were always here.

Show Us a Glimpse of Divine

WHO was the first king of Greece—

    or the first five emperors of China?

How many Louies reigned in France—

    or Caesars in Rome?

Did you know of them?

    What they did?

        How they lived?

    Where they short or tall?

        Did they have any substance at all?

You'd remember Moses,

    Bach, Da Vinci, Aristotle, and Descartes;

You'd remember Alexander,

    But not like Shakespeare or Mozart:

        For you can build the tallest building,

            Live inside the largest house,

                Have all the land and all the food,

                      All the jewels and all the gold;

SHOW US A GLIMPSE OF DIVINE

You can take the seat of power—

and declare yourself a God,

Mint a coin in your honor—

Build a tower like Nimrod;

But, only those will last—

of the kingdom of world's past:

With heart and soul,

And everything that makes us feel;

And dreams that take us into real:

That erase the lines—

of space and time,

And that show us a glimpse—

of Divine;

For no Caesar or Ebenezer—

will ever compare—

to the people who've shared with us—

a vision of a world we can share;

Show Us a Glimpse of Divine

So let us all join hands together—

    with all the world out there,

        And try to better—

           the human condition—

                for us—

                    and our future heirs;

So only those will last—

    of the kingdom of world's past:

        With heart and soul,

           And everything that makes us feel;

        With dreams that take us into real:

           That erase the lines—

                of space and time,

                    And that show us a glimpse—

                    of Divine!

If

IF YOU can use knowledge,

    Perception—

        and understanding—

            to look beyond the illusion of time,

                And all that is composed therein:

                    Energy,

                        Matter,

                            Space;

If you can endeavor to escape—

    the capsule that encloses you,

        And open your eyes—

            beyond sight and sound;

If you can shatter pride—

    and squelch ambition,

        And see the utter futility—

            of striving after that—

                which is merely temporal;

IF

If you can realize—

    the common origin that the world shares,

        And teach your heart—

            to put all of life—

                on a par with your own;

If you can see that black and white—

    are one and the same,

        And love them equally—

           With equity,

                Justice—

                    and judgment;

If you can perceive—

    the utter simplicity of complexity,

        And yet never give way to conception,

            But to the veil of essence—

                which lies behind it;

IF

If you can view your structure—

    as one encased in illusion,

        Yet ascribe value—

            to this transitory existence;

Then:

    The spiritual essence—

        shall course through thy veins,

            And life and death—

                shall be one and the same;

The heavens—

    shall reveal themselves—

        to you in the night,

           And the glory of God—

                shall be—

                    thy Light!

Cherish Her Whole

STEAMY nights,
    Cloudy days,
        Empty mind,
            Heart on fire;

Honey lips,
    Swaying hips,
        You're the victim —
            of your desire;

You can't see the danger,
    Through the flames you've changed you:
        Turning to ashes your virtue;
            Tearing you in half,
                enough to hurt you;

Blind physicality will burn you,
    Objectify and she will spurn you;
        But cherish her soul,
            and she will forever embrace you;

Cherish Her Whole

Look to the mind—

    and see the source of her life;

Seek contentment—

    from her spirit that's inside:

        And you'll always—

            find the woman of your dreams,

            Drawn to her by her charms,

            By the beauty of her soul;

And you will find—

    that it's not her looks,

        But the wisdom—

            of the words that she will find—

            that will draw you—

            into the depths of love:

                A love that's really fine,

                    That will stand the test—

                    of time;

Cherish Her Whole

Be a King,
> Don't be a fool,

Follow your mind —
> and you'll never be blind:
>> You will see the fire —
>>> through the flames of desire;
>> You'll ward off infection,
>>> Contain the light of perfection;
>> Honey lips may amuse you,
>>> But swaying hips won't confuse you;
>> You'll ignite the fire,
>>> The light of your true desire;

Hear her smile,
> Feel her laugh,
>> Hold her closely,
>>> Be her half;

Defend her —
> from the woes that life can bring;
>> Kiss her in the night,

Cherish Her Whole

Love her for her soul;

Feel the warmth—
    from the glow of her love,
        Caress her—
            with your spirit,
                your soul:
                    And you'll always—
                        find this woman by your side,
                            Forever and a day,
                                Until the end of time;

Be a king,
    Don't be a fool:
        Follow your mind—
            and you'll never be blind;

Seek her heart,
    Know her soul;
Shower her with kindness,
    Cherish her whole!

Time

Time—

    Light—

        Life—

Born in a capsule,

    Life with beginning and no end:

        Can't see back to the origin,

            Cannot see the end;

Time:

    It passes by so fast;

There's so much—

    to do,

        To learn,

            To study,

                To envision:

                    To hold the world—

                      in my hand,

Time

To find the reason;

To reach the heavens—

through the light;

Look inside and see,

Time is just an allusion;

Time gives you room to grow,

Room to glow,

So when the capsule ends—

you'll be free:

Prepared for a new journey,

And adorned—

with enlightenment;

Blessed with fulfillment,

And crowned—

with dignity;

Beautified by the will,

And in the presence,

Of God.

If You are There

IF YOU are there—

    can I hear You?

When You are there:

    I feel Your spirit meet mine,

        I sense the sun and the moon,

    You know my thoughts and my dreams,

        You follow me—

            like the one that I love;

You're the cool summer breeze—

    on a hot summer day;

You're the light of the moon—

    when I search for my way;

You're the water,

    The cool, cool water;

You're the reason and the light—

    inside my soul;

If You are There

You are the One,
    You are the sky and the sun;
You are the whistling leaves,
    The spirit of the trees;

You are the One;

You are the air,
    Ah!
        You are the air that I breathe,
           And when I talk to You —
              please answer me!

Yes, you're the cool summer breeze —
    on a hot summer day;

You're the light of the moon —
    when I search for my way;

You're the water,
    The cool, cool water;

If There Are There

You're the reason—

   and the light—

      inside my soul;

When I speak,

   I am half,

      When I listen,

         I am whole:

            You're the reason—

               and the light—

                  inside my soul!

Touch the Sky

Do you dare to take the chance?

    Do you dare to find the way?

Do you want to live your dream?

    Then, envision your life supreme:

        Touch the sky and find the stars,

            Ah!

                The heavens,

                      Just reach out and touch them;

Do you dare to follow dreams—

    that seem impossible?

        Are you scared that you will fail?

            Are you scared that you'll succeed?

            Take the chance!

Visions—

    follow you into the day and the night,

        But you're blinded by your fears:

Touch the Sky

Yes, you're afraid—

to dream,

To act,

To live,

To succeed;

And the pain never leaves—

'cause you hide, it's like suicide;

Giving up on your life—

for a dollar a ride,

And then you're gone;

Watch out for those—

who say you will fail,

They're just afraid you'll succeed;

Listen to Me and stand up,

be strong;

Live well each moment—

and thrive before time—

says you're gone;

TOUCH THE SKY

Dare to live,

    Dare to dream,

        Dare to succeed:

            Touch the sky!

Children of Light

Children of light,

    Fight the dark:

        Don't let it steal —

            the world —

                into the night;

Children of light,

    Fight the dark:

        Fight against wrong,

            Fight for what's right;

People will say

    "you are out of control.

        There is no way,

            You have no say:

                Black is white,

                    White is gray,

                        See our way;

Children of Light

Black is white,

White is gray,

We'll make it okay;"

Listen—

    people will charge into the dark,

        Blinded by the night,

            Afraid of the light;

But—

    You can make a difference,

        you can make it:

           Be a shining light,

                Fight for what's right;

You're the children of light,

    You must fight the dark—

        or the night will reign—

            and the day will die;

Children of Light

You're the children of light,
    Fight the dark:
        Fight against wrong,
            Fight for what's right;

Don't sit back—
    and hide your face from Me;
        Hold on tight—
            until you've set—
                Me free;

Change,
    Change,
        Open up your heart;
Hear my words,
    Hear what I say:
        "Hide from the dark,
            Search for the light;

CHILDREN OF LIGHT

Strive to be noble—

Guardians of Light:

Rays of glimmering sunshine;

illuminating the dawn!"

Valor

Moving round the dark alleyways,

    Sounds of distress,

        Of you, Princess;

I came runnin' 'round the bend—

    to find the Black Knight—

        dressed in my clothes,

            To catch his unsuspecting foes;

Now he's got you,

    Caught by illusions and lies,

        He's the master of deception:

            You could not hide—

            nor turn aside,

            He had you bound—

            for suicide;

You looked at me with those dreamy eyes;

    I saw tears flowing down your face;

Valor

You cried:

   "My love,

      Beware,

         stay away;

   It's a trap,

      Say goodbye,

         Don't let the world pass you by—

            because of me;"

But—

   I cannot leave you:

      I will save you from him—

         or the world's balance will falter;

      I will not hide—

         nor turn aside;

      I'll stay and fight—

         to make things right;

Valor

He wants a world—

    without color or sound:

        Without order or love,

            Without spirit, without life;

He wants a world—

    where silence is a shroud—

        that envelops a desolate earth—

            void of life;

No—

    I will not leave you:

        I will stand against him,

            The world's balance will not falter;

    I will not hide—

        nor turn aside;

    I'll stay and fight—

        to make things right;

Valor

For I'm the voice of reason:

    I will not appease him,

        "Truth" and "Justice" are my names;

    And the sanctity of life,

        The dignity of every being,

            And the grace and harmony—

        of this living planet—

               are mine to protect,

                And duty calls.

Higher

I try—

    to understand my pain—

        when you're gone;

And when you're near,

    I feel—

        the rush of the wind—

            in the storm,

        the rain in my life;

You are my friend, my foe, my mate,

    You push me higher,

        You expect me—

            to compromise,

                To love you,

                    To fight:

            To try—

                to understand your pain—

                    when I'm gone,

Higher

And when you're near,

    To feel—

        the rush of the wind—

        in the storm,

        the rain in your life;

I am your friend, your foe, your mate,

    I push you higher,

        I expect you—

            to compromise,

            To love me,

                To fight,

        To try—

            to understand my pain—

            when you're gone;

And when I'm near,

    To feel—

        the rush of the wind—

        in the storm,

HIGHER

the rain in my life,

In your life,

In our life;

Time in the Sun

Sometimes—

   I think about the days—

      when life was simple—

         and you were in my life:

            Never the time for being sad,

              Only playing and having fun,

            Forever young and in love,

              It was our time in the sun;

I remember the times—

   when the sun—

      shined its light upon the world,

         And the heavens opened up to us;

Whenever I needed someone—

   you were always there:

      I could always count on you,

         In the winter and the rain;

Time in the Sun

With sunshine or with pain,
    You were there to guide me;

I would walk across the world,
    I would wait a thousand years,
I would sacrifice my life—
    if I could save yours;

But now the time has come—
    to say goodbye forever,
        But I can't let you go:
            Life is a shore without a sea,
                Without you,
                    Without your love;
            It feels like we—
                have only just begun,
                    Now time will take you—
                from the sun:
            You are the flower—

Time in the Sun

and I'm the rain;

No goodbyes,

Only love;

Memories of you—

in the sun;

Memories of you in the sun:

Never the time for being sad,

Only playing and having fun;

Forever joy in my heart—

will be the love we shared,

Just you and I,

together,

Always one.

Purple Roses

Here we are bound together —

    by pleasure and pain:

        Holding on to each other —

            'til the sun comes back again;

Purple roses, sweet kisses,

    Velvet embraces,

        In a garden of splendor,

            In a valley of gold;

We are two lovers that meet in the night,

    singing sweet love songs —

        until morning's light:

            Come to me,

                Be with me,

                    Make love to me forever;

            Come with me,

                Lie with me,

                    Fly with me —

Purple Roses

        high—

            on the wings of eternity;

I can hear distant bells call out—

    from heaven to earth,

        To us;

    They send for us, and we are here:

        Together—

            we see earth's—

                thin veiled veneer;

    A love everlasting,

        Forever sincere;

    Drawn to each other—

        with a love so dear;

A life full of hope,

    A room full of lace,

Purple roses, sweet kisses—

    and a velvety embrace;

Purple Roses

The angels, they've blessed us—

    with a saving grace:

        A love for each other—

            that is beyond this place:

        A gift of sentient moments—

            to thoughtfully face;

        And a task of sweet ascension—

            to an eternal embrace!

The Dawn

You are the woman—

    who "looks out like the dawn"[6];

You are the lady—

    of dreams and fairy tales;

You are that someone—

    that I've been searching for,

        Looking for—

            all of my life;

And when I found you—

    I heard—

        the angels sing their love song,

            Saw them dance the dance of love;

I whispered—

    "I love you!"

        and we danced—

            beneath the sun;

---

[6] Song of Songs, King Solomon 6:10

The Dawn

The water and the rain,
    White lilies on the ground,
        The early morning dew,
            Life begins with you;

When I peer into your eyes—
    and embrace your hand in mine:
        Your gaze just fills my soul,
            And your touch just makes me whole;

I love—
    The way you walk,
        The way you talk;
    The face you make—
        when you blink your eyes;
You stimulate my senses,
    Make meaning out of life,
        And I love you,
            My dear,
                With all of my heart!

Share with Me the Silence

People say it's quiet,
> But I know it's not true,
>> 'cause I can hear myself—
>>> thinking—
>>>> about you;

Wherever you are, I'm with you,
> Just listen to your feelings,
>> Just share with me the silence,
>>> Listen to your heart;

I'm with you in the summer,
> In the winter, I'm with you;

The good times I'll share with you,
> The bad times too;

SHARE WITH ME THE SILENCE

Compossible[7], we are together,

   Impossible to be apart;

Just share with me the silence,

   Together—

      Just One heart.

---

[7] Only those substances are compossible that are conceived by God as related within the spatiotemporal and causal structure of a world that is in its richest form. A possible world is made up of individuals that are compossible—that is, individuals that can exist together. Possible in coexistence with something else.

The Promised Land

The wind is blowing,
    The water sparking,
        The band is playing the song —
            of children playing,
                Of people saying,
                    "*How good it feels to be free!*"

The golden clouds up above,
    The birds flying overhead;
The sight of happiness —
    without loneliness,
        Of peace and harmony;

The world moves in rhythm's beat,
    The waves they rise fall,
        To orchestrate a merry few —
            so that we may have it all;

THE PROMISED LAND

The choice is simple—

    for you, for me:

        Good health,

            Good life,

                Sweet dignity;

A miracle true,

    This life at hand,

        If you will just—

            accept God's plan;

It's simple to see—

    For you, for me:

        Stewards for the earth—

            we are meant to be;

So, behold and cherish—

    each grain of sand:

        Then take the til'[8]

            and sow the land,

---

[8] tiller

The Promised Land

Seize the path—

    and take the stand,

        Then lead us to—

            The Promised Land.

A Cool Spring Breeze

The leaves rustle to greet the summer,
    Life blooms everywhere;
The birds have come to sing to us—
    Their love song's in the air;

A cool spring breeze,
    A clear blue sky,
Lying still by clear waters,
    Just you and I;

A cool spring breeze—
    The glow of your eyes,
The patter of raindrops,
    Rose petals lead our way;

The crackle of the fire
    A silhouette in twilight,
The warmth shared between us,
    The taste of heavenly fruit;

A Cool Spring Breeze

Today,

    I will sing you a love song,

        Like birds,

           We'll fly away;

  Sailing—

        the heavens above the sunrise,

          The dawn,

              It lights our way;

Never goodbye,

    No need to tell why,

        Just knowing that we—

            are meant to be—

              together;

Cool and free,

    Fresh breeze by the sea,

        It's blowing at you and me,

           We are three forever;

A Cool Spring Breeze

In the heat of the day,
    Whatever comes our way—
        we'll make beautiful—
            yesterday,
                Tomorrow—
                    and today!

To Create a Work of Art

Each day the world's created,

    Not one is just the same,

Each moment is unique,

    Cherish each with acclaim;

Before you create a work of art—

    take each experience to heart;

        Embrace each moment with sweet caress,

        Take time to see color,

           sound and sense:

        Feel it, measure it, weight it true,

           Next, step back and marvel—

                at life's miraculous—

                and colorful hues;

Then canvas with your heart express—

    truth in pureness,

        Tenderness:

To Create a Work of Art

Add a measure of your soul to share,

Transform the shapeless—

from shadows—

to a beautiful whole,

So fair;

For, to create a work of art,

It must come from the heart,

It must come from that part of you—

you can hardly recognize;

With senses—

the world is illuminated—

for the mind to interpret—

its practical meaning;

But through art—

will your soul express—

its heavenly worth,

Its happiness!

A Familiar Place

The wind whispers to me,
    The trees sway,
        The clouds hang low,
            And, yet, the sun still shines inside,
                I see it in the sparkle of your eyes;

It is the Spirit that surrounds you,
    It is the dawning of a new age;
It is a time to be alive,
    and a brave new world approaches:
        And we must be strong,
            And we must prepare,
                All the flowers are blossoming,
                    A new world is there;

Yes,
    I see it,
        I see it coming,

A Familiar Place

Just stay with me,
    And—
        If we build it together:
            A beautiful harmony—
                and a dignified tapestry,
            A loving place,
                A welcoming place,
                    A caring place;
        Then it shall exist forevermore,
            A world of beauty from aft to fore:
                Togetherness with sunshine,
                    Connectedness with dignity,
                Happiness with prosperity,
                  A garden of splendor,
                A loving embrace,
                  A friendly space,
                A world of soulful sunshine,
                  A Familiar Place.

ALAN RAYMOND FINE

www.ingramcontent.com/pod-product-compliance
Lightning Source LLC
Chambersburg PA
CBHW021018090426
42738CB00007B/823